for The Scholars

FIVE TRADITIONAL SO

arranged by JOHN RUTTE

T0083175

1. THE GIRL I LEFT BEHIND ME

Irish

* or other suitable syllable

girl __ I left be - hind __ me.   Ah

Ah

girl __ I left be - hind __ me.   2. O __ ne'er shall I for - get that night — The

girl be - hind me.   Ah   Ah

girl be - hind me.   Ah

S.
A.   Ah

T.   stars were bright a - bove me, And __ gent-ly lent their sil - v'ry light When first __ she vow'd to

Bar.   Ah

B.

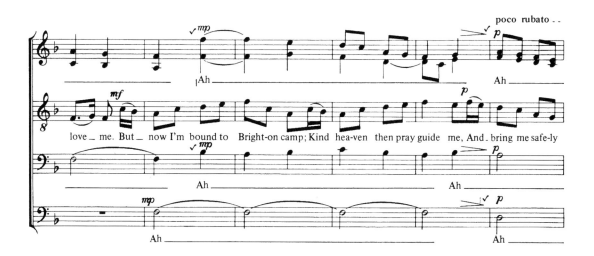

Ah   Ah

love __ me. But __ now I'm bound to Bright-on camp; Kind hea-ven then pray guide me, And __ bring me safe-ly

Ah   Ah

Ah   Ah

2. O WALY, WALY

Somerset

8

deep as the love I'm ___ in: I know not if I sink or ___ swim.

5. O love is hand-some and love is fine, And love's a jew - el while it is

Ah ___

(Hum)

new, But when it is old it grow-eth ___ cold, And fades a - way like morn-ing ___ dew.

3. THE BRITISH GRENADIERS

4. GOLDEN SLUMBERS

17th-century words

Gol - den slum - bers kiss your eyes; Smiles a - wake you when you rise; Sleep, pret-ty wan - tons, do not cry, And I will sing a lul - la - by.

5. DASHING AWAY WITH THE SMOOTHING IRON

18

24

25